Flower Gardening:

ANNUALS

The Gardener's Collection

Better Homes and Gardens® Books

Des Moines

MEREDITH® BOOKS
President, Book Group: Joseph J. Ward
Vice President and Editorial Director: Elizabeth P. Rice
Art Director: Ernest Shelton

ANNUALS
Senior Editor: Marsha Jahns
Editor: Debra D. Felton
Art Director: Michael Burns
Copy Editors: Durrae Johanek, Kay Sanders, David Walsh
Assistant Editor: Jennifer Weir
Administrative Assistant: Carla Horner
Special thanks: Thomas E. Eltzroth

MEREDITH CORPORATION CORPORATE OFFICERS:
Chairman of the Executive Committee: E. T. Meredith III
**Chairman of the Board, President
and Chief Executive Officer:** Jack D. Rehm
Group Presidents:
  Joseph J. Ward, Books
  William T. Kerr, Magazines
  Philip A. Jones, Broadcasting
  Allen L. Sabbag, Real Estate
Vice Presidents:
  Leo R. Armatis, Corporate Relations
  Thomas G. Fisher, General Counsel and Secretary
  Larry D. Hartsook, Finance
  Michael A. Sell, Treasurer
  Kathleen J. Zehr, Controller and Assistant Secretary

*All of us at Meredith® Books are dedicated to providing you
with the information and ideas you need to garden
successfully. We guarantee your satisfaction with this book for
as long as you own it. If you have any questions, comments,
or suggestions, please write to us at:*

MEREDITH®BOOKS, Garden Books
Editorial Department, RW 240
1716 Locust St.,
Des Moines, IA 50309-3023

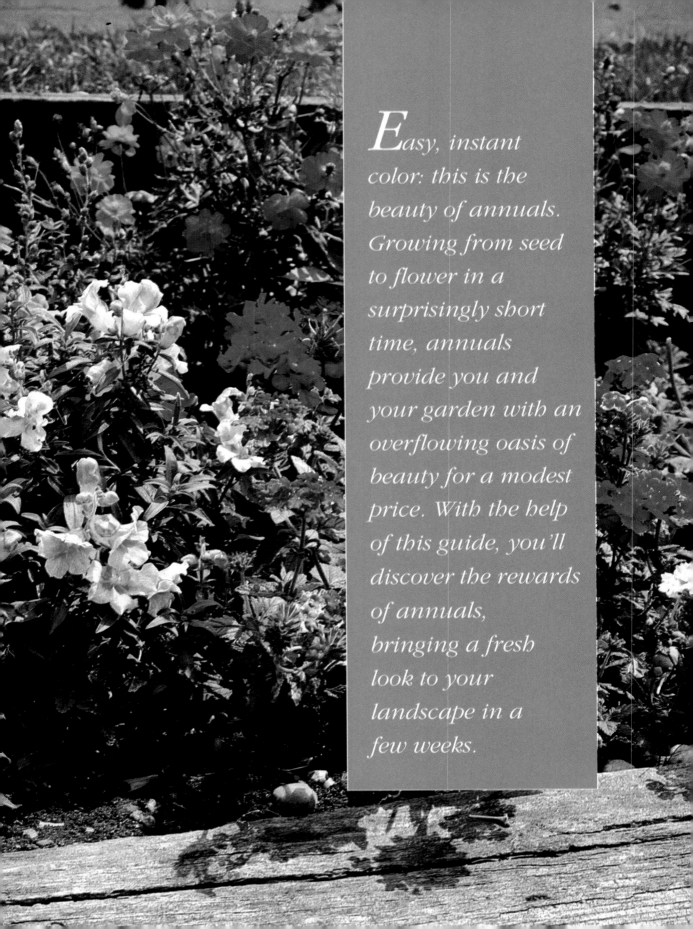

Easy, instant color: this is the beauty of annuals. Growing from seed to flower in a surprisingly short time, annuals provide you and your garden with an overflowing oasis of beauty for a modest price. With the help of this guide, you'll discover the rewards of annuals, bringing a fresh look to your landscape in a few weeks.

CONTENTS

USES FOR ANNUALS 6

DESIGNING WITH ANNUALS 20

PLANTING AND CARING FOR ANNUALS 28

DIRECTORY OF ANNUALS 40

ZONE MAP 62

INDEX 64

Uses for Annuals

*A*nnual flowers are available in an incredible range of colors, shapes, and sizes. Widespread, too, are the uses for annuals in your landscape. With a colorful imagination and an abundant selection of flowers, you can select annuals that will beautify your home and garden quickly and easily

An Abundance of Annuals

Annuals come in an endless array of colors, textures, habits, and sizes. By grouping the flowers in mass plantings, you'll enjoy a rich and bountiful garden all summer long.

In Mass Plantings Because annuals are inexpensive, many gardeners fill an area with dozens—even hundreds—of a single type of annual to create a mass planting. Massing calls for plants with strong visual effects: bright colors, prominent lines, and attention-grabbing textures. Use mixes with a wide range of colors, such as the many warm tones of marigold or zinnia. Or work with a single color, such as hot pink impatiens or petunia. For good verticals, use larkspur or tall snapdragon, and for a striking effect, go with big plants such as castor bean or sunflower.

Large and small areas are naturals for massing. Bold beds in a lawn, wide sweeps along a driveway or property line, shady swaths beneath the canopy of a big tree—all are good candidates for mass plantings. So are smaller areas, such as between the curb and sidewalk or along either side of the front steps or garden gate.

As Edgings and Hedges Trimming the edge of a flower garden with a row of compact, low-growing annuals gives the entire planting a sense of continuity, adds a finishing touch, and visually ties the garden to the lawn or other surroundings. Edgings are useful along driveways, patios, and walkways, where they not only add color but also help soften harsh, straight lines. Neat, compact plants with a long flowering season, such as ageratum, alyssum, wax begonia, and French marigold, are best in edgings. Tall, dense-growing annuals, such as burning bush, cleome, and tithonia, make good temporary hedges or screens.

Though annuals may look like an extravagance, a few flats of flowers are more affordable than trees and shrubs. Plants shown here include pink and white impatiens, petunias, salvia, marigolds, and pansies.

Problem-Solving Flowers

In addition to their beauty in flower beds, borders, and bouquets, annuals provide quick, inexpensive, and simple answers to many landscaping questions or needs—all inside a few packets of seeds.

Create Beauty Borders of mixed annuals around the house will dress it up, while expressing your personality. Highly traveled areas, such as the area around the corner of the garage or a route to the patio, merit special attention and should be spotted with annuals, even if only a few. Your friends will do a double take and share in the luxury as they pass by.

Put the Flowers to Work If your land slopes away too quickly for easy planting, modify the angle with intermediate terraces and a graceful flow of steps. Use railroad ties, timbers, or rocks to reshape and retain the earth, and fill in the pockets with low-growing shrubs and enhancing annuals. An alternative is to plant a strong ground cover that will prevent erosion and then bring life and beauty to the slope by adding the colorful blooms of annuals.

Add Interest Often there's a block of land between the driveway and the entry to the house that suffers from a case of the blahs. Bring it to life with a few shrubs, a few rocks, and a mix of your favorite annuals. A narrow strip between the driveway and the property line can be made a wall of vibrant color with a pattern of annual flowers.

Disguise Problem Areas Take attention from eyesores, such as sheds and trash storage areas, by hiding them behind flowers. And perk up a delicious but unattractive vegetable garden by edging it with annuals or mixing flowers among the rows.

Bedding plants can turn a frumpy front yard into a festival of flowers. Marigolds, dwarf salvia, and two varieties of alyssum fill this traffic-stopping border.

Container Gardening

Annuals in containers are perfect for use on the patio, deck, or porch, where you can treat them like furniture, rearranging them to suit your needs. Even apartment, condominium, and town-house dwellers can grow a colorful garden on a balcony, windowsill, or rooftop.

Which Annuals to Choose For containers, medium-size, low-growing trailing annuals usually look best. Mature plant height should be no more than 1½ times the container height. For greatest effect in small containers, fill them with one type of annual. For mixed plantings, use large, wide containers. Plant as you would a flower bed, with taller plants in the center or behind low growers.

Gardener's Tip

Avoid placing containers where heat becomes intense, such as against a west wall, or in windy locations.

Soften the edges with trailers such as lobelia or verbena.

Choosing the Right Containers Use containers with drainage holes in the bottoms or sides. Good planters are made of clay, ceramic, concrete, plastic, or weather-resistant wood such as cedar or redwood. But let your imagination go wild. Use sawed-off wooden barrels, old wheelbarrows, flue tiles, strawberry jars, or any other container with good drainage.

Growing Mix and Fertilizers A blend of lightweight components is the only practical growing mix for containers. Otherwise, the containers will be too heavy and they won't drain adequately.

Prepared packaged mixes, often sold as planter mixes, usually work well. Or prepare your own mix by blending one-third peat moss or fine-textured composted bark, one-third coarse-grade perlite, one-sixth sifted compost, and one-sixth good garden soil. Moisten the components as you mix them. Before planting, be sure to add dry fertilizer to the mix according to package instructions.

Planting If a drainage hole is large, cover it with screen or other material that will keep the soil from washing out. Fill the container with growing mix to within about 1 inch of its top, gently pushing it down to eliminate any air pockets. Reduce normal spacing between plants by about one-third. (For example, if normal spacing in the garden is 12 inches, decrease it to about 8 inches.)

Immediately after planting, moisten enough so some water leaks from the drainage hole. Keep the top soil moist with frequent light waterings until plants are established, then water when the soil that's 2 inches deep becomes dry.

Care After Planting Pinch your container annuals to induce

Plant containers with compact annuals that produce nonstop color, such as petunias, marigolds, pinks, sweet alyssum, impatiens, and geraniums.

branching, remove faded flowers, and control pests. If you didn't add a controlled-release fertilizer to the soil mix, apply liquid fertilizer every two to three weeks.

Hanging Baskets

Hanging baskets let you elevate garden displays to eye level or above, providing seasonal color and interest to porch and patio overhangs, lampposts, arbors, tree limbs, and other strong outdoor structures.

You can plant a basket with one type of plant only, or mix and match a variety of plants. If you do the latter, be careful not to overdo with too many plant types or colors. Good combinations are (1) begonias, alyssum, and pansies; (2) verbena and geraniums; (3) begonias and browallia; (4) marigolds, alyssum, and lobelia; and (5) petunias, geraniums, and lobelia.

To create a moss ball, fill a wire basket with moistened sphagnum peat moss until the wire is completely covered with a 1-inch-thick layer of moss. Fill the center with a lightweight, well-drained moistened mixture of potting soil and peat or perlite.

Gardener's Tip

Hanging baskets are viewed mostly from the sides or from below, so low-growing and trailing plants are good choices.

Poke holes into the moss all the way around the sides, top, and bottom of the basket, and insert the plants so their root balls pass entirely through the moss lining. Plant the top as you would any container. Keep the sphagnum peat moss, which dries out quickly, moist at all times.

When planting a wooden basket, hold plants in place while adding the potting mix around the roots. Space plants evenly in the basket. Firm the soil and water well.

Secure wires with a pliers to make sure the basket will not fall. You also can use a chain or a rope, as long as it is durable. Hang from a screw eye or cup hook. Continue watering the plants regularly; the soil should not dry more than 1 inch below the surface.

Annuals for Special Uses

Annual flowers are suitable for many special uses. Select the right plants, and you'll enjoy sensory delights indoors and out.

For Climbing and Vining
Climbing annuals swiftly can grow large enough to screen out an unpleasant view, shade a bald plot, enliven a dull corner, or create a secluded nest. Annual vines grow so rapidly that it's unnecessary to do anything but sow the seeds right into the prepared ground. Pruning is rarely necessary. Climbing and vining annuals include morning-glories, nasturtiums, cardinal climbers, and sweet peas.

For Rock Gardens Annuals are an asset to rock gardens because they ensure color until frost. They're especially valuable to fill in crevices until permanent plants take hold, to add a spot of color, or to fill bare spots quickly. They should be low growing, creeping, or spreading into a carpet. Sweet alyssum, lobelia, cornflower, pansies, linaria, phlox, cuphea, torenia, sweet William, nierembergia, 'Swan River' daisy, portulaca, verbena, ageratum, and ice plant all fit the description.

Some annuals like full sun and cool soil. This can be a problem in hot areas; ease it by shading the roots with a rock or decorative mulch, such as wood chips.

For Cutting Whether you're a serious flower arranger or someone who just likes to cheer up a room with fresh-cut blooms, you'll reap rewards from annuals planted for cutting. A separate cutting garden is ideal if your property is large, but well-planned mass plantings and small beds of mixed flowers can double for snipping.

Choose annuals with long, stiff stems and durable blooms. Top-notch choices are aster, cosmos, dahlia, marigold, snapdragon, and zinnia. If you plan to harvest often, plant more than just a few, so their stems will grow strong. Harvest regularly to keep flowers coming.

Treat yourself to a bouquet. This one contains stocks, snapdragons, lisianthus, and celosia.

Annuals for Special Uses

For Fragrance Annuals can be a great source of garden fragrance. Few plants top the delicate sweet scents of alyssum, mignonette, pinks, stocks, petunias, dianthus, candytuft, heliotrope, or sweet pea. Place plants where you'll have the most opportunities to enjoy their fragrance: on the porch, deck, or patio; under a window; near a door or garden gate; or at a spot in your yard you often walk by.

For Drying Sometimes known as everlastings, flowers suitable for drying have a strawlike texture and hold their shape and color all winter without care or water. Choices include: celosia, statice, strawflowers, bells-of-Ireland, ammobium, and globe amaranth. Flower stems should be cut before the blooms are fully open, tied together, and hung upside down in a dark, airy place for two to three weeks.

Nostalgic Mixes You can create the beauty of old-fashioned flowers in any planting pocket that receives at least six hours of sun a day. Mix the clumps so they seem haphazard and not like an army on parade.

Plant taller zinnias, marigolds, and a few cosmos toward the rear as a backdrop, with snapdragons and petunias midway, and pansies and ageratum up front. Use sweet Williams, dahlias, violas, marigolds, and petunias for bright color all summer. For a red-gold mix, try dianthus, marigolds, asters, rudbeckias, and calendulas. Mix statice here and there for garden color and later drying. Focus on two or three colors or a soft blend of pastels.

Or, mix the bold and the wispy. In back, use spikes of hollyhock or larkspur for tall color, softened by the thin-stemmed delicacy of California or Iceland poppies. In front of sunflower plants, mingle gaillardia, forget-me-nots, and dwarf phlox with a carpet of lobelia. Be sure to water them and remove faded flowers.

It makes scents to add fragrant plants, such as these petunias and geraniums, to a garden.

18

Designing with Annuals

You can create the flower garden of your dreams using a variety of brilliant bedding plants. To create interest, blend several colors, shapes, and textures. And to make sure your garden bursts with blooms, design it with careful attention to the sun and water requirements of your favorite flowers.

Design Basics

Beautiful borders must be planned, with a seer's eye to the final pattern and effect. Whether you are a novice or an old pro, you'll find it helpful to sketch the border on paper first. Note the colors and the bloom times.

Planning the Size The size of an annual border can be as long as you want it to be but should only be as deep as your arms can reach. You should be able to tend the flowers at the back without stepping on those in front. If you can place the border where it can be reached from two sides, then it can be twice as wide.

Fitting In Unless your preferences or the architecture of your house dictate a formal garden, an informal approach usually is more pleasing to the eye, and maintenance takes less time. Border edges may be straight or in flowing curves, and the plants within them should be uneven clumps or drifts rather than a stiff arrangement of rows.

Borders may back against a fence or the house or may stand freely along the driveway or in the center of the lawn. Wherever yours will be, blend it with the house and the rest of the property.

Playing with Color A border can be monochromatic, with various shades and tints of one dominant color, but often it is more appealing when one or two colors predominate and are backed up by one or two complements.

So your color scheme will not look like a crazy quilt, plant at least three of one variety per clump. Repeat favorites or accent plants, so the eye will move along smoothly.

Gardener's Tip

Bright, exciting colors will make a garden appear smaller. Cool tones will make it seem larger.

A mixed spring border pops with bright, warm tones of red, yellow, and orange.

Making Your Bed

Nearly every annual flower is suitable for bedding someplace in the garden. There are special considerations to keep in mind to ensure a well-designed profusion of blooms, however.

Height A mixed bed with a building or fence behind it should have the tallest plants at the rear, working down in stages to low plants in front. When the bed is an island, which allows viewing from several sides, place the tallest plants at or near the center, then scale down to the edges.

Nearby Colors Where colors from surrounding plants are neutral, such as evergreens, mix colors and jumble textures to create a carefree look. When annuals are bedded near plants that have pronounced colors (such as flowering shrubs, bulbs, or perennials), harmony of color, size, texture, and design should be the goal.

Spacing Proper spacing will give your bed a full but uncrowded look. Generally, set mounded plants as far apart as their height at maturity; separate erect or linear growers by half their mature height.

Foliage There's a whole world of foliage, so mix sizes, colors, and shapes. Add a few annuals to your border just because of their unique foliage, whether they are splotched coleus or silvery dusty-miller.

Mixed Plants To relieve monotony, mix plants of different shapes. A carpet of lobelia can be backed with a mound of impatiens and an upright rudbeckia. In addition to shapes, consider mixing flower forms. Blend the daisylike shapes of gaillardia, spikes of larkspur, cactus zinnias, bells of petunias, pansy faces, stars of nicotiana, plumes of celosia, and lollipops of cornflowers.

Flower beds should be geared to the existing climate and soil conditions. This garden includes statice, ice plant, daisies, portulaca, and California poppies because these plants favor the dry soil found here.

Made for the Shade

You don't have to sacrifice colorful blooms just because your garden is in the shade. Whether you are looking for color in a dark strip along the north side of your house, or to highlight the dappled sunlight under an open-branched tree, you can design a bed of annuals that will come to your rescue.

What Is Shade There are varying degrees of shade, from soft, dappled sunlight to dense darkness. Many gardeners have yards that contain both extremes, with varying degrees of shade in between.

The amount of shade on a site can change because of many factors, including the time of day and the time of year. If you are choosing a location for shade plants, it's better to find a site that receives sun in the morning, and shade when the sun is most intense in the afternoon. The morning sun will dry the leaves, helping to prevent disease.

Shade Containers For best growth, place containers of annuals in full sun or partial shade. Few annuals grow and flower well in deep shade, but you can take advantage of the portability of containers to produce blooms for deeply shaded areas. Start by choosing shade-tolerant plants. Grow them in a partially shaded spot until flowering begins, then move them to deeper shade. After a couple of weeks, move the plants back to partial shade to encourage them to rebloom.

Best Shade Annuals Reliable shade loving annuals include browallia, which has small blooms; coleus, with large and colorful leaves; and impatiens, which provide color from summer through fall. Others are lobelia, which is compact and spreading; vinca, a bushy annual with glossy leaves and colorful flowers; and wax begonia, which blooms all season.

Pink and salmon impatiens bordered with lobelia share a shaded flower bed with sweet William and giant marigolds.

Planting and Caring for Annuals

There's more to the pleasure of annuals than bright, colorful blooms. They're also simple to plant and tend, making your job easy all season long. Using the tips on the following pages, you can start the flowers from seeds or bedding plants, then encourage abundant blooms, creating a garden of carefree delights.

Seeding Indoors

You can grow most annuals from seed easily. The size of seed and its sprouting time dictate whether you should sow seeds indoors or outdoors. If the seeds are less than ⅛ inch across, sow them indoors.

Containers They may be makeshift, such as a cut-down milk container. Or, for consistently better results, use one of the many devices made just for the purpose, such as peat pots or plastic flats. The container should be at least 2 inches deep.

Germinating Medium The medium should be sterile and well drained. It may be purchased ready to use or made at home with peat or milled sphagnum moss and fine perlite or vermiculite in a 50–50 mixture. Don't use soil from the garden, and don't reuse the germinating medium; neither will be sterile.

If the container is made of peat or fiber, it must be wetted thoroughly before use, or it will act as a wick and pull moisture from the sowing medium. After the container is completely moistened, place a layer of gravel or newspaper in the bottom to ensure good drainage.

Seeding Fill the flat with moistened medium to within ¼ inch of its top. Tap to remove air pockets; refill if needed. Make rows ¼ inch deep, 2 inches apart. Drop seeds in a row, spacing them so they almost touch. Cover the seeds to twice their thickness with sowing medium or clean, coarse sand. (For tiny seeds, simply press them into the medium without covering.) Label the rows and water gently from the bottom if possible.

Place the flat in a plastic bag, or cover it with a pane of glass to keep the humidity high. This will decrease the need for watering, which can dislodge seeds before they sprout.

Place the flat in good light but not full sun until the seeds germinate. Or, set the flat on top of the refrigerator for a continuous supply of gentle heat.

Transplanting to Pots When the first seedlings sprout, remove the cover and place the flat in an indoor spot that receives full sun, keeping the soil slightly moist. Apply liquid fertilizer at one-fourth strength when seedlings are ½ inch tall. After two sets of true leaves form, shift the seedlings to individual pots of compressed peat moss or sanitized small flower pots. Water gently; place in a cool, shady spot (still indoors). After a couple of days, move back to full sun. Apply half-strength liquid fertilizer after two weeks.

Sow small seeds indoors in flats of sterilized mix. Then shift seedlings to individual small pots after two sets of true leaves form.

Moving Out Four to six weeks after shifting seedlings to individual pots, move them out into full sun on mild days but bring them in at night. Give the seedlings a half day of sun the first three or four days, then increase the exposure. After seven to 10 days, leave them outside full-time in a sunny location. After about two weeks, transplant them to the garden.

Gardener's Tip

Most annuals should be started indoors six to eight weeks before the last predicted spring frost in your area. Begonia, coleus, dianthus, impatiens, lobelia, geranium, pansy, petunia, salvia, and snapdragon will take longer.

Seeding Outdoors

Sowing seeds directly in the garden is useful for large seeds that usually sprout and grow quickly and for types that don't transplant well. Sowing in the garden also works well later in the year when the soil is warm.

garden to a depth of 8 to 10 inches. Run the tiller across the first rows to break up soil even more. This method works well when starting a new flower bed.

1. Good soil preparation is the key to a thriving, colorful annual garden. If you have a tiller, you can eliminate hand-spading and till the

2. Prepare the seedbed by incorporating organic material such as peat moss, compost, or manure; perlite or vermiculite for added porosity; and fertilizer. Work in the material, apply water, and rake smooth. Seeds will not germinate and grow in compacted, lumpy, or dry soil.

Gardener's Tip

To test the soil for planting readiness, squeeze a handful of it. If it stays together, it is too wet for you to work.

4. After the seedlings have developed two or three sets of leaves, you'll need to thin them. Carefully remove seedlings so that you don't disturb the others. Leave space between plants. After thinning, remove the cords you used to define the area.

3. Lay pieces of cord or clothesline on the ground to outline a design within the flower bed. Sow seeds evenly over the ground; cover slightly with soil. Keep moist by watering with a gentle spray from a sprinkler or hose until strong growth appears.

5. Thinning allows your plants to grow to their ultimate size and shape. In a short time, your garden will look like this warm array of cosmos, zinnias, and marigolds. If you remove the thinnings carefully, you can transplant them to another part of the garden or give them to friends.

Transplanting Annuals

Purchased flats of summer annuals can transform a backyard almost overnight, and they're available in a wide array of colors and varieties. Although bedding plants may be more expensive than starting plants from seeds, they'll reward you with at least one extra month of color.

1. When you shop for bedding plants, look for compact, bright green, healthy plants. The label will tell you about variety, color, and height. Don't reject those that aren't in bloom; all-green plants often do better in the long run.

2. If you can't plant right away, keep your new flowers moist. To remove the plants from the pack, hold them with one hand while inverting the pack. If they don't fall out easily, tap the bottom with a trowel.

3. If the plants are not in individual cells, separate them gently by hand or with a knife just before planting; don't allow roots to dry out. Soil in the planting bed should be tilled, enriched, and watered before planting.

4. If roots seem compacted, loosen them gently before planting. Dig a hole slightly larger than the root ball, and set the plant in place at the same level it grew before. Firm soil around the roots.

5. Water well immediately after planting; water frequently until plants become established and new growth has started. Once new growth begins, plants fill in quickly.

Gardener's Tip

If you can't plant your new annuals right away, water daily. There is little medium around their roots, so they dry out quickly.

Care and Maintenance

If a garden full of annual flowers is your goal, your care and maintenance program will assist Mother Nature in producing a garden spot covered with color and life.

Weeding and Mulching Keep the garden free of weeds, not only for the plants' health, but also for their appearance. The best—and simplest—preventive is a good mulch, which not only limits the growth of weeds but also keeps the ground cool, conserves moisture, and is a neat finishing touch. Try bark, wood chips, straw, hulls, or fabric weed block.

Feeding To keep your plants in top shape and full color, give them a monthly feeding of a dry 5-10-5 fertilizer or a solution of soluble fertilizer. A slow-release fertilizer makes the task easier. You feed only once, at the start of the growing season, and the food is released throughout the summer as needed. No other food should be used with slow-release fertilizer.

Supports Plants such as larkspur, hollyhock, and standard snapdragon are so tall and weak they will not stand straight on their own. For these, use a metal, wood, or bamboo stake next to the plant. Tie the flower to the stake.

Vining plants, such as morning-glories, need a wooden trellis or a netting fastened between two posts. Don't worry about tying them—they climb unaided. Avoid growing vines on wires because wires get hot in the sun and can burn tendrils and new growth.

To get exhibition-size flowers on long-stemmed plants, remove all but the central flower bud with tweezers, a toothpick, or your fingertips.

Watering If it does not rain, water most annuals deeply once a week. Thoroughly moisten the entire bed, not just the plants, because dry soil nearby will pull water away.

Shallow watering only leads to poor root systems that stay near the surface of the soil. These cause the plants to dry out too quickly. If the

Many annual flowers, such as marigolds, should be removed as they fade. This simple procedure, called deadheading, ensures maximum and continuous blooming all summer. Clip or snap off dead flowers.

Petunias can get leggy. To keep them compact and to induce more blooming, pinch them back by removing stems at leaf joinings. You'll also encourage growth by regularly cutting flowers for indoor bouquets.

weather is extremely hot or your soil is sandy, you may need to water more often. However frequently you water, never apply less than 1 inch of water at a time.

Gardener's Tip

If possible, water annuals in the morning on days with a sunny forecast so foliage will not stay wet too long.

Multiplying Your Annuals

To get more mileage out of certain plants, grow them in the garden during the summer and indoors during the winter. The best way to do this is with root cuttings that you clip in midsummer. Not only will you have plants to enjoy indoors during cold months, you also will have sizable starts for next spring. The easiest plants to manage in this dual role are coleus, wax begonia, geranium, and impatiens. Take only as many cuttings as you will be able to handle indoors.

1. For best results, clip a stem about 4 inches long with at least four leaves. Remove the lowest two leaves, and apply a rooting hormone to the stem's bottom.

Gardener's Tip

Take cuttings in midsummer to reshape overgrown annuals and ensure a fall flush of bloom for many plants.

2. Insert the cutting into a growing medium of premoistened sphagnum peat moss and/or sand. Place the pot in a plastic bag and set it in an area with good light but not direct sun. In about 10 days, check for rooting by gently pulling on the cutting.

3. When cuttings have rooted, remove them from the rooting medium and transplant them in containers or in the garden, depending on the time of year.

Directory of Annuals

Growing annuals allows you the freedom to change your mind and your color scheme every growing season. No matter what growing conditions you have, there are annual flowers to meet your needs. Make your selections from the array of annuals on the following pages, and enjoy sensational color all season long.

AGERATUM
Ageratum sp.

(also called flossflower)

Description: Long-lasting, fuzzy ¼ to ½-inch blossoms on plants 3 to 6 inches tall (a few reach 2 feet). Blue, white, and pink. Varieties: 'Summer Snow,' 'Blue Mink,' and 'Royal Blazer.'

Light/Soil: Full sun. Will tolerate some shade. Tolerant of all soil conditions.

The low, dense mounds of ageratum are favorites in edgings, window boxes, and other containers.

Planting: Start 6 to 8 weeks early indoors, or buy transplants. May be replanted in late summer in mild areas.

Comments: Use plants for edgings, borders, rock gardens, or pots.

ALYSSUM, SWEET
Lobularia maritima

Description: Fragrant, small-petaled blossoms on compact plants 2 to 6 inches tall. White, rose, and blue. Varieties: 'Rosie O'Day,' 'Violet Queen,' 'Royal Carpet,' 'Carpet of Snow,' and 'Sweet.'

Light/Soil: Full sun. Will tolerate some shade. Tolerant of all soil conditions.

Planting: Sow seed outdoors as soon as ground can be worked, or buy transplants. Often self-sows.

Comments: Use for edgings, borders, rock gardens, hanging baskets, and window boxes. In warm climates, will bloom all year. Trim to encourage new growth.

AMARANTH
Amaranthus caudatus

(sometimes called love-lies-bleeding or tassel flower)

Description: Long, red tassel-like flowers on plants 3 to 6 feet tall. Colorful leaves on some varieties. Varieties: 'Illumination,' 'Early Splendor,' 'Molten Fire,' 'Love-Lies-Bleeding.'

Light/Soil: Full sun. Tolerant of all soil conditions.

Planting: Start seeds indoors 6 weeks early, or plant outside after all frost danger passes.

Comments: Easily transplanted. Likes long, hot growing season. Use as a background plant in a mass planting or against a wall. Drought resistant.

ASTER
Callistephus chinensis

(also called China aster)

Description: Blossoms vary from 1 to 5 inches across. Height, color, and flower shape vary with hybrid. Sizes from 8 inches to 3 feet tall.

Light/Soil: Sunny or lightly shaded location. Rich, well-drained soil.

Planting: Start seeds indoors 6 to 8 weeks early, or plant outside after frost danger passes.

Comments: Mix with other plants. Tall varieties can be leggy. Plants have shallow roots and do best when mulched. Late-summer bloomer—end of July. Susceptible to fungal disease. Heavy feeder. Rotate to a new location each year.

BEGONIA, WAX
Begonia x semperflorens-cultorum

Description: Everblooming single and double varieties on shrubby plants 6 to 8 inches tall. White, pink, and red.

Light/Soil: Almost any light condition. Blooms well in shady areas. Loose, rich soil.

Planting: Start indoors 4 to 6 months in advance, or buy plants.

Comments: Plants do not compete well with other annuals, so mass them alone. Use as a pot plant year-round. Take new cuttings from houseplants in early spring for your own bedding supply.

BROWALLIA
Browallia sp.

(also called amethyst)

Description: Petunialike blossoms. Size varies. Heavily borne on dense plants. Blue, white, and violet. Varieties: 'Blue Bells Improved,' 'Silver Bells,' and 'Velvet Blue.'

Light/Soil: Full sun or partial shade. Tolerant of all soil types if kept moist.

Planting: Sow indoors 4 to 6 weeks early, or buy transplants.

Comments: At end of season, cut back plants and put in pots on a sunny windowsill for winter blooms.

BURNING BUSH
Kochia scoparia trichophylla

Description: Dense, globelike, light green, finely cut foliage plants that reach 3 feet in height. Foliage turns bright red in fall. Variety: 'Childsii.'

Light/Soil: Full sun. Tolerant of all soil types if kept dry.

Planting: Start early indoors, or sow in the garden after the soil warms dependably in spring. Self-sows in mild areas.

Comments: Use plants to make temporary hedges. Try growing in tubs. Tolerates heat and wind.

CALIFORNIA POPPY
Eschscholzia california

Description: Single- and double-flowered, cup-shape, long-stemmed flowers with lacy foliage on 1- to 2-foot stems.

Light/Soil: Full sun or partial shade. Light, well-drained soil.

Planting: Scatter seed outdoors as soon as ground can be worked. Often self-sows.

Comments: Try planting in areas where other annuals won't do well or in tubs and pots. Likes cool weather.

CANDYTUFT
Iberis sp.

Description: Hyacinth-shape white flowers on 10- to 15-inch spikes. A globe-shape variety is available in both dwarf and taller forms. Globes come in different colors. Varieties include 'Umbellata Dwarf Fairy' and 'Hyacinth Flowered Iceberg.'

Light/Soil: Full sun. Some shade in hot climates. Almost any loose soil.

Planting: Sow as soon as ground can be worked. Sow seed every 2 weeks for constant bloom. Sow in fall in mild areas for winter color.

Comments: After first flush of bloom, trim plants back to stimulate flowering. Grow for early cut flowers. Flowers are heavily perfumed.

CANTERBURY-BELLS
Campanula sp.

Description: 2-inch urn- or bell-shape flowers on stems 2 feet tall. Mixed colors. Some varieties have a bell inside a bell.

Light/Soil: Full sun. Rich, moist soil.

Planting: Sow 4 to 6 weeks early indoors, or plant seeds outdoors as soon as ground can be worked. Occasionally self-sows.

Comments: Some varieties are biennial. Blooms in 6 months. Likes cool weather.

CARNATION
Dianthus sp.

Description: Double flowers, 2 to 3 inches across. Florist types borne on wiry stems 16 to 24 inches high; bush forms are 12 to 14 inches high. Bicolors, whites, yellows, and reds.

Light/Soil: Full sun. Light soil kept moist.

Planting: Sow indoors 10 weeks before last frost. Will last several years in mild climate.

Comments: Use bush varieties as bedding and edging plants. Keep cutting both types for continuous bloom.

CASTOR BEAN
Ricinus communis

Description: Tropical, large green palm-leaf plants grow to 10 feet. Leaves are 1 to 3 feet long. Young leaves are red-brown on some varieties.

Light/Soil: Full sun. Rich, moist soil.

Planting: Sow 6 to 8 weeks early indoors, and set outdoors after weather is warm.

Comments: Use as a background plant. Seeds are poisonous, so clip off before maturity. In warm climate, can survive several years.

CELOSIA
Celosia cristata

(also called cockscomb)

Description: Striking flowers 2 to 12 inches in width; shaped like tall plumes or close fanlike clusters.

Celosia comes in both plumed and crested forms. Both are available in a wide range of mostly warm colors.

Plants are 1½ to 2 feet tall. Mixed colors, some intense. Dwarf forms to 8 inches tall.

Light/Soil: Full sun. Cannot grow in partial shade. Tolerant of all soil types.

Planting: Start 6 to 8 weeks early indoors; sow outdoors after frost danger passes, or buy bedding plants.

Comments: Use dwarf varieties for edgings or borders and tall varieties for mass plantings. Flowers keep color after harvest; good in dried bouquets. Drought tolerant.

CHRYSANTHEMUM
Chrysanthemum sp.

Description: 2- to 3-inch, single and double, daisylike flowers on 2-foot stems. Colors vary. Dwarf varieties to 10 inches with 1-inch flowers. Varieties include 'Golden Raindrops' and 'Palvdosum.'

Light/Soil: Full sun but will tolerate some shade. Rich, moist soil.

Planting: Plant seeds outdoors when ground can be worked.

Comments: Use as edging and background plant. Cut for fresh bouquets.

COLEUS
Coleus x hybridus

Description: Foliage plants with occasional white or blue spike flowers; 6 inches to 2 feet tall. Leaves in almost endless colors and mixtures.

Light/Soil: Indirect light or shaded area in rich, well-drained soil.

Planting: Sow seeds outdoors when ground is warm, or buy transplants.

Comments: Use as an edging plant or in pot as accent. Easily carried over winter as a pot plant from cuttings. Pinch to keep bushy.

CORNFLOWER
Centaurea cyanus

(also called bachelor's button)

Description: 2-inch, fine-petaled zinnialike flowers on stems 1 to 3 feet tall. Many colors. Varieties: 'Blue Boy,' 'Pinkie,' 'Snowman,' and 'Jubilee Gem.'

Light/Soil: Sunny location. Does best in well-drained soil.

Planting: Sow outdoors in early spring. Sow in fall about 4 weeks before frost for blossoms before summer heat. Sow in late summer in warm climates.

Comments: Use smaller varieties in rock gardens and borders and taller ones for cut flowers.

COSMOS
Cosmos sp.

Description: 3- to 4-inch daisylike single and semidouble flowers. Feathery fernlike foliage forms a shrublike plant 4 to 6 feet tall. Mixed colors. Varieties: 'Dazzler' and 'Radiance.'

Light/Soil: Sunny location but tolerates shade. Light, partially dry soil.

Planting: Start outdoors after frost danger passes. Often self-sowing.

Comments: Use as a background plant or temporary hedge. Cut flowers for fresh arrangements.

Directory of Annuals

DAHLIA
Dahlia hybrids

Description: Single, double, and semidouble 2- to 3-inch flowers on plants 12 to 20 inches tall. A few tall varieties 3 to 5 feet in height with 4- to 5-inch flowers, but most taller varieties are grown as perennials.

Light/Soil: Full sun. Rich, well-drained soil kept moist.

Planting: Start seeds 6 to 8 weeks early indoors, and set outside after frost danger passes.

Comments: Use dwarf varieties as bedding plants. Taller varieties often need to be staked. Cut flowers of all varieties for fresh arrangements.

DUSTY-MILLER
Centaurea cineraria

Description: Silvery white, fernlike foliage on plants 12 to 15 inches tall. Flowers are small and insignificant.

Light/Soil: Full sun. Well-drained soil.

Planting: Best to buy transplants.

Comments: Use in edges, borders, and rock gardens. Provides good color contrast and variety.

FEVERFEW
Chrysanthemum parthenium
(also called matricaria)

Description: 1- to 2-inch chrysanthemumlike flowers on 2-foot stalks. Dwarf varieties reach 10 inches. Yellow, gold, and white. Varieties: 'Golden Ball' and 'Snowball.'

Light/Soil: Sun or partial shade in hot areas. Does best in rich, well-drained soil.

Planting: Sow 4 to 6 weeks early indoors, or sow outside after frost. May overwinter in warm areas.

Comments: Cut flowers for fresh arrangements. Often used by florists. Taller varieties can be perennials.

FLAX
Linum sp.

Description: 2-inch single flowers on grasslike stems 18 to 24 inches tall. Red, blue, violet, pink, and white.

Light/Soil: Full sun. Well-drained soil.

Planting: Plant seeds outdoors in early spring or fall in warm climates. Sow every 3 to 4 weeks for continuous bloom.

Comments: Difficult to transplant. Use in beds or borders.

FOXGLOVE
Digitalis sp.

Description: 2- to 3-inch-long bell-shape flowers on spikes, 2½ to 6 feet tall. Pink, purple, rose, white, and yellow—with darker mottling inside. Varieties: 'Foxy' and 'Excelsior.'

Light/Soil: Full or partial shade in rich, well-drained soil kept moist.

Planting: Start seeds 6 to 8 weeks early indoors; set out when soil can be worked. Often self-sowing.

Comments: After first flowering, cut main spike to encourage more blooming. If heavily mulched, can often be overwintered to second season.

GAILLARDIA
Gaillardia pulchella
(also called blanket flower)

Description: 2-inch daisylike flowers, single and double varieties to 18 inches tall. Dwarf forms to 14 inches. Reds, yellows, creams, and bicolors. Varieties: 'Tetia Fiesta' and 'Lollipops.'

Light/Soil: Full sun. Almost any garden soil. Takes dry conditions and heat.

Planting: Sow seed indoors 4 weeks before frost goes out of ground.

Comments: Use plants in window boxes and other hot areas. Cut for fresh-flower arrangements.

GAZANIA
Gazania rigens

Description: 4-inch daisylike flowers 6 to 12 inches tall. Cream, red, bronze, orange, yellow, and pink—with contrasting centers.

Light/Soil: Full sun. Shady, light soil that's kept dry is best.

Planting: Start seeds indoors 5 weeks early.

Comments: Use in hot areas. Can take tough conditions. Flowers close at night and on cloudy days.

Gazania is grown for its daisylike flowers on short stalks above a low foliage mound.

GERANIUM
Pelargonium sp.

Description: Versatile group with both single- and double-flowering varieties ranging from 4-inch miniatures to 5-foot "trees." Some scented, with leaves smelling like mint, nuts, rose, lemon, and apple. Some ivylike vine varieties. White, pink, red, and bicolor. Varieties: 'Sprinter,' 'Carefree,' and 'Colorcade.'

Light/Soil: Full sun, but can take partial shade. Well-drained soil.

Planting: Sow seeds indoors 10 to 12 weeks early, or buy transplants.

Comments: Use all varieties as bedding, as well as pot, plants. Use ivy varieties and scented types in hanging baskets and patio tubs. Overwinter cuttings on a sunny windowsill. Treat as a perennial in warm areas. Use hairpins to fasten stems of ivy geraniums to the soil, encouraging growth close to ground.

GLOBE AMARANTH
Gomphrena globosa

Description: ¾-inch cloverlike blossoms on plants 12 to 18 inches tall. White, red, and pink.

Light/Soil: Full sun. Tolerant of all soil types.

Planting: Sow seeds indoors 4 to 6 weeks early or outside after frost danger passes.

Comments: Use in fresh and dried arrangements. Plant in beds, borders, or window boxes. Drought resistant.

GYPSOPHILA
Gypsophila sp.
(also called baby's-breath)

Description: ¼-inch rounded flowers on branched stems 15 to 24 inches long. White or pink. Foliage is finely cut. Varieties: 'Covent Garden White' and 'Rose.'

Light/Soil: Full sun. Does best in poorer soils.

Planting: Plant early outdoors. Sow seeds every 3 to 4 weeks for a continuous supply.

Comments: Provides a light, airy contrast in the garden. Cut for fresh arrangements.

HELIOTROPE
Heliotropium sp.

Description: Large 6- to 12-inch, lilaclike clusters of small, heavily perfumed flowers on plants 1 to 2 feet tall.

Light/Soil: Full sun or light shade. Rich, well-drained soil.

Planting: Sow seeds midwinter indoors, or buy transplants.

Comments: Use plants in borders, patio tubs, or window boxes. Overwinter cuttings as houseplants.

HOLLYHOCK
Alcea rosea

Description: Varieties include single, double, semidouble, and frilled flowers 3 to 4 inches in diameter on stalks 2 to 6 feet high. Mixed colors. Varieties: 'Silver Puff' and 'Majorette.'

Light/Soil: Full sun. Tolerant of a variety of soil conditions.

Planting: Sow 8 weeks early indoors; place outside after night temperatures warm. Shelter from wind.

Comments: Use plants along fences or buildings, or in the back row of flower beds. Some will overwinter one season in mild climates.

IMPATIENS
Impatiens balsamina
(also called garden balsam)

Description: 1- to 1½-inch cup-shape flowers on small, mounded plants 6 to 8 inches in diameter.

Petals are sky blue with white centers.

Light/Soil: Sun or partial shade in warm areas. Prefers light well-drained soil.

Planting: Sow seeds as soon as ground can be worked. In warm areas, sow seeds in the fall.

Comments: Use as a ground cover or as bedding or edging plant. Try mixing with flowering bulbs.

LARKSPUR
Consolida sp.

Description: Single and double flowers borne on spikes 1 to 4 feet tall. Lacy green foliage. Blue, rose, salmon, pink, and white. Varieties: 'Dark Blue Spire,' 'White King,' and 'Pink Perfection.'

Light/Soil: Full sun, but needs some shade in hot areas. Light, well-drained, fertile soil.

Planting: Sow in early spring outdoors. In milder areas, sow in fall. Sow at 3-week intervals for continuous bloom.

Comments: Cut flowers for fresh arrangements. Use plants along fences and walls.

LINARIA
Linaria sp.

(also called baby snapdragon)

Description: Small flowers that resemble snapdragons on 12-inch stems. Finely cut foliage. Bicolors with reds, yellows, and lavenders. Variety: 'Fairy Bouquet.'

Light/Soil: Full sun. Tolerant of all soil conditions.

Planting: Scatter seeds in the fall or early spring outdoors. Not heat resistant.

Comments: Use in rock gardens and borders. Mass plantings best.

LOBELIA
Lobelia erinus

Description: ¼ to ½-inch-wide flowers on small plants rarely over 6 inches tall. Trailing varieties vine up to 2 feet. Blue, white, and pink. Varieties: 'Bright Eyes' and 'Sapphire.'

Light/Soil: Sun, but needs some shade in hot areas. Not heat resistant. Moist, well-drained soil.

Planting: Sow seeds indoors 6 to 8 weeks early, or buy transplants.

Comments: Use plants for edgings, borders, and ground covers and trailing varieties in hanging baskets and pots. Cut back after first flush of bloom for new blossoms.

LUPINE
Lupinus sp.

Description: Small 1- to 2-inch, clustered flowers on spikes 1 to 3 feet tall. Blue, pink, lavender, yellow, white, and bicolors.

Light/Soil: Full sun, but shade in warm areas. Not heat resistant. Rich, moist, but well-drained, soil.

Planting: Sow seeds early outdoors. In mild climate, resow in the fall.

Comments: Cut flowers for fresh arrangements. Trim off old flower spikes to encourage new growth.

MARIGOLD
Tagetes sp.

Description: Double 3- to 5-inch blossoms on plants 6 inches to 3 feet tall. Foliage is finely cut—often with a pungent scent. Dwarf varieties have single or double blossoms 1 to 2 inches across. Cream, yellows, and reds.

Light/Soil: Full sun. Almost any rich, well-drained soil.

Planting: Start seeds indoors 6 to 8 weeks before last frost date or outdoors after frost danger passes. Or buy transplants.

Comments: Use dwarf varieties in borders, edges, or tubs. Mix tall varieties with other flowers or plant in mass.

MORNING-GLORY
Ipomoea sp.

Description: Tubular flowers on vines that grow to 10 feet. Flowers may be white, pink, red, blue, purple, or chocolate brown; some varieties produce multiple colors. Flowers open in morning, fade by midafternoon.

Light/Soil: Locate in full sun, in well-drained soil.

Planting: Sow directly in the garden after all frost danger passes, or start seedlings indoors 4 to 5 weeks earlier.

Before sowing morning-glory seeds, soak them in water for 10 hours, or nick the hard seed coat with a file.

Comments: Avoid overwatering or overfertilizing, which produces vine at the expense of flowers. Some varieties need coaxing to begin climbing.

NASTURTIUM
Tropaeolum majus

Description: 2-inch single and double blossoms on plants 8 to 15 inches tall. Climbing variety reaches 6 feet. Shiny, rounded, green leaves. Mixed colors and bicolors.

Light/Soil: Full sun. Likes sandy soil but will grow almost anywhere if soil is kept dry.

Planting: Plant seed outside after frost danger passes.

Comments: Will flower more abundantly in poorer soils. Use leaves as tasty, colorful additions to salads. This annual seems to thrive on neglect.

NICOTIANA
Nicotiana sp.

(also called ornamental tobacco)

Description: Tube-shape blossoms 2 inches in diameter on plants 1 to 3 feet tall. Large basal leaves. Crimson, rose, lavender, pink, and white.

Light/Soil: Full sun; some shade in warm areas. Tolerant of all soil types. Heat resistant.

Planting: Start 6 to 8 weeks early indoors. Seed is slow to germinate. In mild climates, sow outside.

Comments: Use with border plants. All varieties are heavily perfumed.

PANSY
Viola sp.

Description: 1½- to 3-inch overlapping flowers on low, spreading plants 8 inches tall. Wide range of colors. Noted for dark, central, facelike markings on petals.

Light/Soil: Full sun but will need partial shade in hot areas. Rich, moist, but well-drained soil.

Planting: Sow indoors 10 to 12 weeks early to get blooms in late spring. Or buy transplants. Sow midsummer for plants that can be overwintered for early spring bloom.

Comments: Use as edging plants or in bulb and rock gardens. Keep cutting flowers to stimulate growth. Pinch back young plants to encourage branching.

PETUNIA
Petunia sp.

Description: Many shapes, sizes, and colors on plants 1 to 2 feet tall. Singles, doubles, and semidoubles. Common garden petunia (*P. x hybrida*) has blossoms 2 to 3 inches across.

Light/Soil: Full sun to partial shade. Rich, well-drained soil kept moist.

Planting: Sow seeds indoors 6 to 10 weeks before last frost, and set out plants after frost danger passes. Or buy transplants.

Comments: Use as border plants or in pots and tubs. Try cascade varieties in hanging baskets. Pinch back plants after first blooms to encourage branching.

PHLOX
Phlox drummondii

Description: 1- to 1½-inch blossoms clustered on plants to 15 inches tall. Dwarf varieties reach 8 inches. White, red, pink, and blue. Varieties: 'Blue Beauty,' 'Crimson Beauty,' and 'Pink Beauty.'

Light/Soil: Full sun; can take light shade. Can take almost any well-drained soil.

Planting: Sow seeds indoors 4 to 6 weeks early, or sow directly outside after frost danger passes.

Comments: Use plants in borders, window boxes, and rock gardens. Keep old flowers clipped off to stimulate new growth.

Directory of Annuals

PINK
Dianthus sp.

Description: 1- to 2-inch single, double, and frilled flowers on plants 8 to 12 inches tall. Reds, white, and bicolors. Varieties: 'Bravo,' 'Queen of Hearts,' 'Hybrid,' 'China Doll,' and 'Baby Doll.'

Light/Soil: Full sun. Light soil kept moist.

Planting: Sow 6 to 8 weeks early indoors, or sow outside after frost danger passes. May survive winter.

Comments: Use as edging plants. After first flush of bloom, cut back to encourage new flowering. Some are fragrant.

POPPY
Papaver sp.

Description: 2- to 5-inch silky, crepe-paperlike, cup-shape flowers on 1½- to 3-foot stalks. White, red, pastels, and bicolors. Varieties: 'Iceland,' 'Shirley,' and 'Oriental.'

Light/Soil: Full sun. Tolerant of all soil conditions.

Planting: Sow late fall or early spring outdoors. In warm climates, blooms all winter. Seedlings do not transplant well. Mix seeds with sand when planting for better spacing.

Comments: Use in mass plantings. Make good cut flowers if harvested when buds just begin to split open.

PORTULACA
Portulaca grandiflora

(also called moss rose and sun plant)

Description: Single and double 1-inch blossoms on creeping plants that reach 7 inches tall. Foliage is dark green and needlelike. White, red, rose, yellow-orange, and lavender flowers.

Light/Soil: Full sun. Almost any well-drained soil.

Planting: Sow 6 weeks early indoors, or outside after frost danger passes. Mix seed with sand before planting for better spacing. Often self-sows.

Comments: Use these hardy plants in problem areas, beds, rock gardens, or out-of-the-way nooks.

RUDBECKIA
Rudbeckia sp.
(also called gloriosa daisy)

Description: Large, single, daisylike flowers on stalks 18 to 24 inches tall. Flowers have brown centers with yellow, orange, or bronze petals.

Light/Soil: Full sun, but can tolerate partial shade. Well-drained soil.

Planting: Sow seeds outdoors in late fall or early spring. Plants often self-sow.

Comments: Trim back flowers to encourage new growth. Cut flowers for fresh arrangements.

SALVIA
Salvia splendens
(also called scarlet sage)

Description: 1- to 2-inch tubular flowers clustered on spikes. Plants are b14 to 20 inches tall; dwarf varieties are 12 inches. Deep scarlet, pink, blue, and white.

Light/Soil: Full sun or partial shade. Rich, well-drained soil.

Planting: Start 6 to 10 weeks early indoors, or buy transplants.

Comments: Use plants in beds, borders, and patio tubs. Bright colors can be almost overpowering.

SNAPDRAGON
Antirrhinum majus

Description: 1- to 3-inch tubular flowers heavily clustered on spikes. Plants grow 6 inches to 3 feet tall. Mixed colors. An open-face variety is available.

Light/Soil: Full sun. Rich, well-drained soil.

Planting: Sow seeds 6 to 8 weeks early indoors, or buy transplants.

Comments: Use dwarf varieties in rock gardens or borders. Try tall varieties in bed backgrounds. Pinching will stimulate growth.

STATICE
Limonium sp.

Description: ¾-inch blossoms borne on bare 16- to 20-inch angular stems, rising from a basal rosette of leaves. Blue, lavender, rose, and white flowers.

Light/Soil: Full sun. Almost any well-drained soil.

Planting: Sow 6 to 8 weeks early inside, or outside after frost danger passes.

Comments: Use flowers in dried bouquets. Blossoms hold color well. If seeds are encased in husk, break before planting.

STOCK
Matthiola incana.

Description: Small, many-petaled flowers on spikes. Plants 1 to 2 feet tall. Common color is deep blue,

Plant stock where you can enjoy the delightful fragrance. Give plants full sun where temperatures are cool; partial shade otherwise.

but rose, white, and pink also areavailable.

Light/Soil: Full sun; partial shade in hot areas. Moist but well-drained soil.

Planting: Start 6 weeks early inside, or outside as soon as ground can be worked. In warm climate, sow in fall.

Comments: Use in beds. Cut the heavily scented flowers for fresh arrangements.

STRAWFLOWER
Helichrysum bracteatum
(also called everlasting)

Description: 2- to 3-inch daisylike, double flowers on 2-foot stalks. Red, salmon, purple, yellow, and white.

Light/Soil: Full sun. Tolerant of all soil types if kept dry.

Planting: Sow inside 6 to 8 weeks early, or outside when soil warms.

Comments: Use in both fresh and dried bouquets. Dried flowers hold color well.

SUNFLOWER
Helianthus annuus

Description: 3- to 14-inch-diameter, daisylike blossoms on plants 2 to 10 feet tall. Yellow, orange, mahogany, and bicolors. Varieties: 'Teddy Bear,' 'Sungold,' 'Mammoth,' and 'Red.'

Light/Soil: Tolerant of all soil types kept moist. Full sun.

Planting: Sow seed outdoors after frost danger passes.

Comments: Use tall varieties as temporary screens. Try smaller varieties in beds. Grow large varieties for tasty seeds.

SWEET PEA
Lathyrus odoratus

Description: 1- to 2-inch bonnet-shape flowers on climbing plants 20 to 30 inches tall. A dwarf bush type reaches 15 inches tall. All colors (except yellow), plus bicolors. Petals of different varieties may be ruffled or plain.

Light/Soil: Full sun or partial shade. Rich, well-drained soil kept moist.

Planting: Sow outside as soon as soil can be worked. In warm climate, plant in fall; mulch. Vining types need early support.

Comments: Soak seeds. Use an inoculant of nitrogen-fixing bacteria coating on the seeds before planting. Use in beds or window boxes. Enjoys cool weather; does not flourish where summers are hot.

SWEET WILLIAM
Dianthus barbatus

Description: Small, compact plants 4 inches to 2 feet tall with flat, closely packed flowers. Bicolors, reds, and whites. Varieties: 'Wee Willie,' 'Red Monarch,' and 'Summer Beauty.'

Light/Soil: Full sun. Light soil kept moist.

Planting: Sow 6 to 8 weeks early inside, or buy transplants. Blooms a second summer in mild climates.

Comments: Use as a border and rock garden plant.

TITHONIA
Tithonia sp.

(also called Mexican sunflower)

Description: 3- to 4-inch sunflowerlike blossoms on 4-foot-tall plants. Orange-red flowers with light centers.

Light/Soil: Full sun. All soil types. Drought resistant.

Planting: Sow 4 to 6 weeks early inside, or outside after frost danger passes.

Comments: Use bushy plants as temporary hedges. Grows quickly in hot weather.

VERBENA
Verbena x hybrida

(also called vervain)

Description: Flat clusters of small flowers 2 to 3 inches wide on plants 6 to 10 inches high but spreading up to 2 feet wide. Many bicolors with white centers.

Verbena

Light/Soil: Full sun. Rich, well-drained soil, kept moist. Heat resistant.

Planting: Sow seeds 10 to 12 weeks early inside, or buy transplants.

Comments: Use as fragrant ground cover or edging and in window boxes or rock gardens. In warm climates, will act as perennial.

VINCA
Vinca sp.

(also called periwinkle)

Description: 1½-inch single phloxlike blossoms on rounded, bushy plants 1 to 2 feet tall. Rose, pink, white, and bicolors.

Light/Soil: Full sun; partial shade in hot areas. Well-drained soil.

Planting: Sow seeds 12 to 15 weeks early inside, or buy transplants.

Comments: Use as a border plant or in pots and tubs. In warm climates, treat plants as perennials.

VIOLA
Viola sp.

(also called violet)

Description: Small 1- to 1½-inch, pansylike flowers on compact 8-inch plants. Blue, yellow, red, white, apricot, and purple.

Light/Soil: Full sun, but needs shade in hot areas. Rich, moist, well-drained soil.

Planting: Sow inside 10 to 12 weeks early for blooms in late spring. Plants started midsummer can be overwintered for spring bloom.

Comments: Use in edges and rock gardens. Plants flower longer than pansies, a relative.

ZINNIA
Zinnia sp.

Description: Dahlialike blossoms 4 to 7 inches across on plants 2 to 3 feet tall; rounded, pointed, or cactus-type petals. Round blossoms 1 to 2 inches across on plants 6 to 12 inches tall. Mixed colors and bicolors.

Light/Soil: Full sun. Tolerant of all soil types.

Planting: Start seeds 6 to 8 weeks early indoors, or outside after frost danger passes.

Comments: Use dwarf varieties in borders, rock gardens, or window boxes. Try all varieties in mixed beds or planted alone.

Zone Map

The key to successful gardening is knowing what plants are best suited for your area and when to plant them. This is true for every type of gardening. Climate maps, such as the one opposite, give a good idea of the extremes in temperature by zones. By choosing plants best adapted to the different zones, and by planting them at the right time, you will have many more successes.

The climate in your area is a mixture of many different weather patterns, sun, snow, rain, wind, and humidity. To be a good gardener, you should know, on an average, how cold the garden gets in winter, how much rainfall it receives each year, and how hot or dry it becomes in a typical summer. You can obtain this general information from your state agricultural school or your county extension agent. In addition, acquaint yourself with the miniclimates in your own neighborhood, based on such factors as wind protection gained from a nearby hill, or humidity and cooling offered by a local lake or river. Then carry the research further by studying the microclimates that characterize your own plot of ground.

Here are a few points to keep in mind:

■ Plants react to exposure. Southern and western exposures are sunnier and warmer than northern or eastern ones. Light conditions vary greatly even in a small yard. Match your plants' needs to the correct exposure.

■ Wind can damage many plants, by either drying the soil or knocking over fragile growth. Protect plants from both summer and winter winds to increase their odds of survival and to save yourself the time and energy of staking plants and watering more frequently.

■ Consider elevation, too, when selecting plants. Cold air sweeps down hills and rests in low areas. These frost pockets are fine for some plantings, deadly for others. Plant vegetation that prefers a warmer environment on the tops or sides of hills, never at the bottom.

■ Use fences, the sides of buildings, shrubs, and trees to your advantage. Watch the play of shadows, the sweep of winds, and the flow of snowdrifts in winter. These varying situations are ideal for some plants, harmful to others. In short, always look for ways to make the most of everything your yard has to offer.

THE USDA PLANT HARDINESS MAP
OF THE UNITED STATES AND CANADA

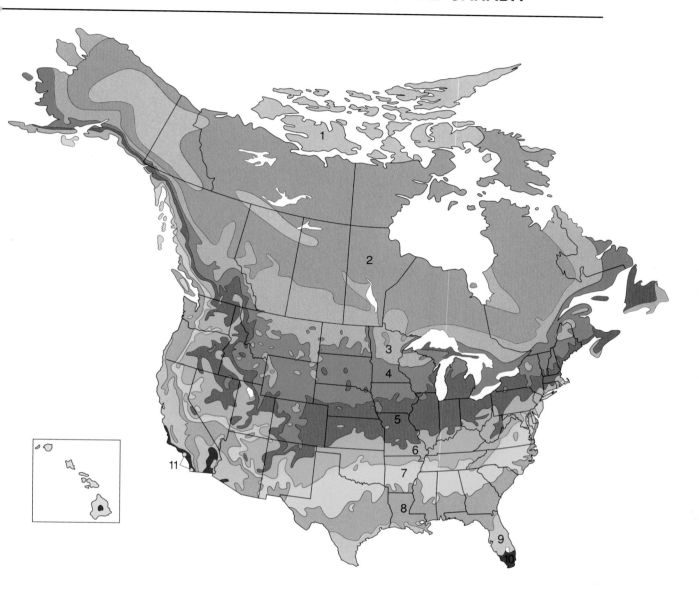

RANGE OF AVERAGE ANNUAL MINIMUM
TEMPERATURES FOR EACH ZONE

	ZONE 1	BELOW -50° F
	ZONE 2	-50° TO -40°
	ZONE 3	-40° TO -30°
	ZONE 4	-30° TO -20°
	ZONE 5	-20° TO -10°
	ZONE 6	-10° TO 0°
	ZONE 7	0° TO 10°
	ZONE 8	10° TO 20°
	ZONE 9	20° TO 30°
	ZONE 10	30° TO 40°
	ZONE 11	ABOVE 40°

Index